Floods and Flowers

The poetry of

Kaitlyn Grace Hoagland

First Edition

Published by Kaitlyn Grace Hoagland

ISBN 979-8-9999919-0-4

Printed in the United States of America

To my Lord and Savior, Jesus Christ,
who not only sits with me through floods,
but continues to grow flowers within me.

Poetry can change the world because it can change people.

K.G.H.

Contents

Dear Reader,

This book did not start out as a book. It began as a girl
with longing and dreams and nowhere to put them.
Poetry has been the act of coming back to myself when
I lost her along the path of growing up. It began softly
one day, a silent poem. And then another, and another,
and another. Until suddenly, I found my voice again
and she refused to be quiet any longer.

Poetry has been my outlet and the most precise way of
seeing how I feel, how I see the world, and who I am. It
has allowed me to cope with the life I thought I
wanted, and the life I lost. Looking back, it is easy to see
the hands of God throughout this process, and I am
reminded of what Jesus says in John 13:7. Without
struggle and pain beyond belief, I would have never
picked up a pen.

I share my words with you not for fame or recognition,
but in hope they inspire you, as the words of other
poets have inspired me. I don't write for the public, for
approval, or for what would sell books or fill billboards.
I write for myself and for God.

In this process, I've discovered my innermost self beneath all the masks and cobwebs. Writing has given me power and purpose. It would be easy to tuck these poems away and never share them, as I have done until now. But given the freedom I have found, I feel I must share this with you. Poetry has shaped and changed me, and I hope it will do the same for you.

This is only the beginning for me. These poems are just the start of my writing journey, and my newfound perspective of life. To see where I once was and where I am now is truly a testament to the Lord's faithfulness. I am excited to see where my next path leads. But for now, there is no more to add to this story. It is complete. It is finished. And it is time to share it.

A piece of my heart,
K.G.H.

The Flood

When breathing felt like bleeding
and surviving felt like dying

The Pain That Stays

There is comfort in my pain
He is always there for me
When joy slips away
And trust is broken
When happiness fades
And innocence is stolen

He saves me a seat at the table
And asks me to recall
The memories that allow him rulership
A position gained
Through propaganda and deceitful nurturing

I run back to him
Because unlike others in my life
He doesn't leave
So pain will stay
Because you did not

I hold onto pain
Because he holds onto me
He holds me close
And never leaves

He is the only constant
I've ever known
He makes me feel seen
Yet never truly whole

When joy visits
He waits in the corner
Watching me
Anticipating my arrival
And when joy abandons me
As she always does
I return to pain
My umbrella in the rain

There is comfort in my pain
Not because he heals me
But because he knows
How to keep me wounded
An unfortunate prize
Grand and all-inclusive

There is comfort in my pain
At least he knows my name

K.G.H.

I'm Fine

I have a tendency
To take care of everyone around me
Yet never myself

I don't give myself grace
When I have a bad day
Like I do others
I don't tell myself it's okay
Like I tell them

How can I treat everyone around me
With the utmost sympathy
Yet turn my head
To the girl inside me
Begging for help?

Maybe it's because I help others
That they think I'm fine
That I have it all together
Do they not see the warning lights
Behind my reassuring eyes?

Maybe they just think it's a glow

The sparkle of a girl
Who has it all together
Maybe I try to fix the people around me
So my life feels somewhat stable
As long as everyone around me is happy
I think
Then I'll be okay

Yet my outside circumstances
Could never dictate my peace
No matter how wonderful they might be
And I would know

I try to perfect the world around me
Yet not the one inside me
I run away from the construction of my heart
And bite my lip with false hope in my eyes
So everyone will turn their head from me
And I will not draw any speculation
About my shortcomings

I cannot be seen as broken
Only strong and helpful
I must be on a pedestal for all around me

They can look up and see my daunting presence

Yet not close enough to see
That the glow in my eyes are tears
And my heavy breathing is not from the elevation
But from the overwhelming anxiety
That I cannot seem to shake

I feel like I have to be
The example
The compass
The one who holds it all together
Even when I'm still learning
Who I am

I carry strength like a requisite
Inherited and invisible
As if being understood
Is nowhere near the importance
Of being dependable

Some days I feel like a child
Pretending to be a woman
Offering certainty and security

I've never truly had

Maybe it's an eldest daughter quality
To put everyone's needs above your own
And sacrifice your well-being
My mind tells me not to break, not an inch

No one can see the pain inside of me
What a disappointment I will be
Who will they look up to if not her?
If she can't handle it, how can I?

No–
Hold it together for everyone else
Instead of taking the time
To take care of yourself

K.G.H.

I Miss the Girl I Was

I'm starting to forget you
But I don't think I want to

You brought out my inner child
And the girl I always wanted to be

I'll be fine without you
But I miss who I was
When you said you loved me

As your memory fades
And your absence solidifies
I morph back into a stone-cold warrior
Instead of the soft, lover girl I was becoming

I wish you were still around
Who knows what I might have been?
Maybe not an angel
But perhaps a flower of some sort

I miss the girl I was with you
But you took her away from me

K.G.H.

A Hedgehog's Dilemma

I yearn for you in the cold

And you, I

A reciprocated love is delightful and rare

I burn for the warmth inside of you

It is beautiful and refreshing

And somehow, you long for mine

We make our way towards one another

I love our calculated steps and playful banter as we go

I do enjoy a good conversation

However, a dreadful fear approaches

A realization I want to deny

My sharp spines would surely wound you

If we decided to deepen our intimacy any further

A shallow pool it must remain

Instead of my intended roaring ocean

Your quills would impale me straight through

If you took another step

Why must loving you be parallel

With killing you?

Why does holding you lead to a prophesied

destruction?

Why can't I touch you without a knife in my hand?

Maybe this is our curse

To love one another

No matter how much it hurts

K.G.H.

Maggot

I never knew you as a little boy
When you were scared of the dark and had a favorite
toy
I only know you as the man that you've become
And I wonder where in your life had this sense of anger
come from?
A sense of entitlement and defensiveness
A sense of rage and then negligence
Does it eat at you like it does me?
Do these memories grip at your throat until you can't
breathe?
Or does it feel like a moral obligation
To maintain superiority through grief and
domination?
I don't know why you are so at ease to bring me sorrow
Is it a part of your insecure and demeaning motto?
I think my love for you is your greatest asset
It feeds your ego
But eats at mine like a greedy maggot

K.G.H.

Silk-Wrapped Dreams

I keep my dreams tucked away
In the deepest corners of my mind
Because while they may never come to pass
They can never be destroyed
By the cruelty of this world
I keep them hidden
Because my imagination is often kinder
Than my reality

My dreams are like a gift
Wrapped in a beautiful box
With a silk ribbon
It will never be opened
Because I fear that
Like my heart
Once someone sees its true colors
They will be disappointed
In who I really am
And the ruse will be up
And their hopes put to rest
I keep it hidden
Because it cannot be frowned upon when unraveled
It can only be desired from a distance

It will leave people wanting more
Wanting to know what it's really like on the inside

So that is enough for me
Not to follow my dreams
Because keeping them hidden
Is safer than being seen

K.G.H.

Drowning Love

I fear if I reveal the truest parts of myself to you
You will cast me out in fear like they always do
You see, most people say I don't have love in my soul
But that is only because I hide it
Before it grows out of control
I love too big and too quick every time
And attach myself to a new love
Like they have always been my lifeline
And long ago, when I was a child it was fine
As I was too young to know of deceit and lies
But now I'm all grown up, yet still a child at heart
So I build a fortress around my feelings
And shut them down from the very start
Do you now see the frustration I feel
When you ask me why I don't love you?
It is as if my love is blocked by a dam
And it is cracking
Until it breaks and destroys you
I've yet to meet anyone who can handle
The love that I bestow
Most people's cups only fill to the top
And don't delight in overflow
So instead of experiencing

Another rejection and heartbreak
I will construct a wall around my heart
Before it is too late
Because if I give you all of me
And my love drowns you
It will end up killing us both
As a river needs water too

K.G.H.

Communication is Key

Communication is key
And you changed the locks
I always question your obsession with doorbells
And you wonder why I never knock

We play the same song
In different bands
We speak sign language
With different hands

We wouldn't make it far
In a three-legged race
You're much too fast
And I'd struggle to match your pace

You're also a man who doesn't know what he wants
Unless it's toying with a girl until she likes you back
Only to leave her exposed and defenseless
In an all-out ambush attack

Communication is key
And you changed the locks

K.G.H.

The Tedious Vase

She's the second choice
She's second place
She trips and falls before
She can pick up the pace

It's a shame that
She will never win the race
She'll never be the flowers
But always the vase

And not the shiny either
Or the painted, ceramic one
No, she is bland out of fear
For the flowers cannot be outdone

But she holds them together
Until they wilt away
She will soon be a new home
To yet another self-absorbed bouquet

Who needs a vase that won't stray
It sits quietly as it decays
It has no legs and nowhere to go

So it sits unfulfilled as a two-faced foe

Because she hates it here
And the life she lives
She plays victim
To the hand that was entirely hers to give

She looks down upon herself daily
And every time she's cast aside
Her rage builds silently

She's a puppy in a purse
She's always second best
Maybe even third
If she had to guess

You would think it was just this time
A selfless friend
An unreciprocated lifeline

But no–
She looks back and shrieks
Realizing that she's always been the entourage
And never the peak

And it's not that she desires to put others down
Constantly one-upping them
Until their face holds a permanent frown

She just wants a friend
That's a friend
Not a political move
Or a rebound clique
She yearns for genuineness
The kind of trait that doesn't have to try
It just exists

K.G.H.

An Ill-Fated Dance

Love is a dance
And I try not to step on your feet
My hands are shaking but
I hope that my beautiful blue dress
Takes your gaze away
And into a world
Where we watch movies with our children at night
A world that is much simpler
Than the one we were born into
One where men like you end up with women like me
The politicians and executioners watch us warily
As we waltz around the shining dance floor
I look over your shoulder and all around
But you tell me to look only in your eyes
Deep brown beauties that pierce into my mind
And thoughts and soul
With you, right here
Everything is simple
Everything is perfect
I wish that we could live in this moment
I wish that it was enough
But we must return back to reality
Where I step on your feet

And my fear of monsters
Keeps me from intertwining my soul with yours
For the remainder of my mortality
Love is a dance
And I seem to sabotage the steps
No matter how hard I try

K.G.H.

Butterflies in My Stomach

I used to have butterflies in my stomach
Entrapped in my ribcage, they made a home
I never asked for a pet, but for once
It was nice to not feel so alone

I've never been one to let something go
And I tend to hold onto things tighter than most
Even when you left
My company was an empty seat
A ghastly companion

You took the keys with you
The keys to my insides and to my heart
With nowhere to go and your absence solidified
Those poor creatures were starved of nurturing
And suffocated in the dark

Their lifeless, dead bodies fell to the bottom of my
stomach
And the acid didn't mix well with their rotting
carcasses
My repressed feelings were bound to come out one way
or another

Although, I have to say
I really thought they would be freed by your command
And not my gag reflexes

My body never recovered
My health quickly declined
I guess that's just one of the consequences
Of trapping everything on the inside

My quiet obsession killed my soul
And it seems my body too
I was poisoned by your counterfeit love
It turned my heart black and my skin blue

The dogs now eat my vomit
And the birds pick at my pale flesh
I'm nothing but a distorted spirit now
One filled with restless torment

Shall I spend my days haunting
Or perhaps as a guardian angel?
At least eternity grants me enough time
To try and understand your betrayal through every
angle

I used to have butterflies in my stomach
Thriving, beautiful, and full of life
But your abandonment and my insanity choked their
tiny necks
And stabbed their hearts with sharp knives

                                        K.G.H.

The Arduous Truth

I have a scar on my finger
A trench in my thumb
Because I swallow my feelings
Until I am numb

Is it because I am a woman
Or because I am young
That you feel entitled
To the breath in my lungs?

Respect should be reciprocal
Not something you inherit
It's earned through gentleness, understanding
And honorable merit

There is a hole in my tongue
From the careless way I bite it
Seething with rage
But too drained to fight it

For years I tried to be heard
And fought for the arduous truth
But you took advantage of me

And blamed it on my youth

I wish I was brave enough
To say this to your face
But I care too much about you
To put you in your place

K.G.H.

A Simple Confession

Heart pounding

Fingers shaking

Muscles retracting

Tears falling

I laugh at how I'm reacting to a simple confession

And yet it is everything to me

You told me that you loved me

Heart pounding

Fingers shaking

Muscles retracting

Tears falling

I laugh at how I'm reacting to a simple confession

And yet it is everything to me

You told me that it was all a lie

K.G.H.

How Do I Wait, God?

I read in the Bible to wait for You
To surrender to Your timeline, and Your plan
Not mine
And I understand that, I really do
Because as impatient and greedy as I am
I know that Your ways
Are higher than my ways
And Your thoughts
Are higher than my thoughts

I know You have a plan
And purpose for my life
I believe that You love me
And work all things for good
For those who love You
But what do I do
When I wait
And You decide to stay silent?

How can I be still
When life never stops moving?
When battles must be fought
And responsibilities must be taken care of?

What about when choices must be made
And I don't know what to do?
When I don't feel prepared or ready
And I must make a move
How do I wait?

Life goes on every single day
And You don't rush to make deadlines
I know that
I know that You are the Most High King
The Creator of the very world
That tries to run me in circles

How do I wait, God?
When my mind and body betray me daily
And I pray and fast and follow You
When I read Your Word and fight my flesh
Only to find no relief

How do I wait, God?
When I see everyone around me building rockets
And flying into space
And I am still chained to the ground

How do I wait, God?
When I have hard decisions to make
Choices that will affect
The very outcome of my life
And I call to You and don't hear Your voice

How do I wait, God?
When I've been broken down
By the weight of the world
Barely crawling atop it
And am not spared from my suffering

I know You are perfect
I know You are faithful
And I know that You know my pain and desires
More than anyone else ever could
But how do I wait, God?
When I feel life pass me by
When I know that my days are numbered
And I feel completely stuck

How do I wait for deliverance?
How do I wait for healing?
Why does my future self get her dreams

And I don't?
Am I not as lovable?
Am I not deserving like she is?
Don't You see
The daily breaking of my heart
And the invisible tears
That flow from my soul?

Why are You quiet?
Can't You give me anything?
A break
A breakthrough
A sign
A whisper
A healing
A taste of magic

I don't know how to wait
For what I don't know is coming
When You have gone quiet
I fear You aren't there
That You've forgotten me

Please, God
Teach me how to wait
So I can be free

K.G.H.

The Current

~~

The storm was over
but the damage still remained

Growing Pains

As the eldest daughter
I'm the first to leave the nest
And it hurts
To be on my own
All alone
Yes, it's freedom and independence
But growing up has forced me
Out of the only home
I've ever known
While my parents and sister still remain
Their lives go on
But I'm the one that's changed
I visit like a stranger
Or a guest
Just a visitor that stops by
On occasion
When schedules align
But I think I liked it better
When time was a circle and not a line
And we were all together in the same home
Growing up can be bittersweet
When you're the first one to go

K.G.H.

Seventeen

You look in my eyes
But it's no longer me
The girl that you're looking for
Is young and naive
I've grown up
But she's still seventeen

K.G.H.

Merry-Go-Round

I'm an awkward adult wearing a child's clothing
Suddenly I'm twenty years old
And I don't know who I am
So I step in pattern with who I've always been
And what I've always done
An adolescence that I've outgrown
Childish habits that I cannot seem to break
Because I don't know who I am without it
Without my high water jeans and ¾ length cardigan
I clasp my fingers tightly around the scraps she left
behind
The girl I am no more
A woman now, can that be?
I don't know her
And she doesn't know me
Yet I'm terrified of becoming
Another round of refining and molding and sculpting
I'm in middle school all over again
Where fear and embarrassment and failure and change
were on the to-do list
And staying the same was irrelevant
I yearn for it all the same
Maybe even more now

But I'm terrified to fall into the sky
When I know I'm safe on the ground
I've played this game too many times to not level up
To not increase the difficulty and embrace the
challenge
I'll go mad spinning in a circle forever
When I know there are dreams waiting to be lived
Once I get off this merry-go-round
If I ever get off this merry-go-round
I have to get off this merry-go-round
It's time to get off this merry-go-round

K.G.H.

Stay With Me

Knowing you can't go back

To a time or a place

Once you're safe

Once you've figured it all out

Makes you try to soak it up all the more as you go

But how torturous it is

That I am not the mysterious future

Nor the film of my adolescence

I sigh as I try to grasp it

To hold on

Even just for a second longer

Stay with me

But the air slips through my fingers

And my body ages

And my mind races

With the notion

That I can never go back

Or hold on

Stay with me

I say

As I see the next coming of dawn

K.G.H.

Me vs. Me

Why is it so hard to be myself?

Shouldn't that be

The easiest thing in the world?

Why do I fight who I am

And hate her for it later?

Why do I shame my innermost parts

But feel miserable as the girl I conform to be?

I want to be beloved

And I want to be myself

My brain knows it's an unreasonable request

Can someone tell my heart that?

K.G.H.

What Winter and I Have in Common

I hate the dry cold that the winter brings
I have never longed for it, only warmth
My pale skin and cold-natured body yearn
For the sun and the life it brings
My frigid soul aches for it too

I hate the brittle cracking of dead wood
In an airless, freezing frost
I hate being confined to a building
Of four walls and synthetic heat

I wish my body could thrive in this weather
Like it does in the summertime
Maybe I would like it more
If I could lay in the grass on a new morning
One with the dew and frost
If I could see the ice run away as the sun returns
If I could feel an icy breeze
And not flinch or shiver
At its gut-wrenching shrill

Then maybe I could enjoy the dark cold
That is often misunderstood

Maybe I could finally understand myself
And love her too

Because truthfully
The winter is misconstrued
It's often quiet and seldom adored
If people would just give it a chance
If they would look up
And see the white crystals
That fall from the sky and wonder why
Maybe they would give thought
To people like me

Misunderstood and cold
With whispered beauty all around

K.G.H.

Knots

Why did you have to mess everything up by liking me?

Why couldn't you just see me as a friend like every
other guy always has?

You've ruined it

My stomach is in knots

And I am acting like a child

No one has ever liked me

I've gotten so used to one-sided romance

That I find anything else grotesque

Don't find me pretty

Don't enjoy my conversation too much

Or I'll have to let you go

I wish I could accept it

But who are we to reject the status quo?

K.G.H.

Two Truths and a Lie

I want you

I miss you

I need you

K.G.H.

Terrified and Trying Anyway

I know a lot of times
I don't try my best
Or give my all
Or go all in
Because that takes vulnerability

It takes courage to say
"This is my attempt at life–
The maximum version of myself"
It's scary because that's it
What if people look up at my ceiling and frown?
What if it's not enough?

I keep my talents hidden
Just so people can't hold it over me
They'll have to wonder what it would be like
They'll never truly know
And I guess living in this way
I'll never know either

But I'm learning
That hiding doesn't protect me
It just keeps me small

And I don't want to be small anymore

                                    K.G.H.

The Open Door

You left abruptly
You left like a father
Running from the mess he made
Craving a fresh start
You left the door open on purpose
You left like you would come back
You even kissed me goodbye
What am I supposed to do with that?

You left your favorite jacket hanging by the door
And it blends into the background with each passing
day
It hangs like a dead man's weight
Heavy and hollow and full of decay
I stare at it from the couch most nights
And every time it rains I think of you
Wondering if you will ever come back for it
Or if you're wearing a different one
With someone new

Your spot in the driveway is still empty
The pebbles don't know what to do
With air to breathe and freedom to be seen

The weeds gradually overthrow where your tires once
sat
Making a home for themselves
Delighting in the midst of all this
I walk around that barren space
And I never park there
Just in case you return
Old wounds reopen
As new fires burn

You left the door open
It lets a bitterness in and all of my warmth out
But I never dare to touch it
Just in case
And every time the wind blows, I look up
The hairs on my arms rise
My breath abandons my lungs
And my brain replays my favorite film—
The one where you walk back through the door
And say that you left it open on purpose
You're sorry it took so long
But promise it was worth it

You left your coat because you knew

You'd be back before the rain came
You left the door open because you knew
You would be back before it closed
And you left for a good reason
To get me that necklace I'd always wanted
A heart shaped locket, engraved in gold
You clasp it around my neck
And ask me to open it eagerly
On the left, a red camellia
And to the right, a yearning question
Can I be yours?
It took you so long
Because of your attention to detail
It had to be perfect for me
And everything is perfect
And it all makes sense
Until

The door slams shut
A storm brews outside
Violent and unforgiving and irreversible
The winds pick up
As nature grows impatient
Weeds greedily devour

The empty space that used to be your own
Your jacket collects dust
And the door remains closed
I jolt back to reality

You never knew what to get me
You always picked up last-minute roses and chocolate
Am I no more than a statistic to you?
A bland mirror of every woman you ever knew?
You never cared to ask
You didn't know how much it meant to me
A simple necklace with such intimate intricacy
You never researched the flower
Or what it symbolized
You wouldn't know the subtle difference between
Can I be yours? and *Would you be mine?*
But I think that's pretty evident
By the way you treated me
You never saw yourself settling down
And I only saw you as the man I wanted you to be
You left the door open, knowing I'd be waiting
With my wagging tail beating the floor
You saw me as your well-trained dog
Obedient, with my tongue out on all fours

You left the door open
Assured that I'd be waiting for you
You left me a few treats behind
A betrayal I can't subdue

The hard truth about an open door
The maddening thoughts and ghastly visions I once
adored
The cruel waiting and false hope
Your absence is the loudest silence I've ever known
And what hurts the most
Is that you left it open on purpose
Knowing that I would wait for you and think of you
In the summer I burned the brightest red
And in the winter I became the deepest blue

The winds have closed the door on you
They turned the lock and bolted it through
They gave me closure you didn't have the decency to
award
They saw through the hollow lie you failed to defend
The inevitable laws of nature have acted against you
Your time in this house has come to an end

K.G.H.

My Greatest Enemy

Who gave her the right to be so mean?
Why do her opinions always belittle me?

I think she tries to ruin my day
And bring me down with the words she will say

She is so negative, it is unbearable
Even when I try my best, I still feel terrible

She's never happy with what I do
No matter the outcome, she always disapproves

I am done giving her power over me
So I walk away from the mirror and decide to finally be
free

K.G.H.

Starting Over

It's hard to start over
After all we've been through
I don't know why people think I'm able
To unlearn everything about you

It's hard to start over
Even if I wanted to
I don't know how I can forget what we had
And be open to something new

It's hard to start over
Willing, with a clean slate
I look for you in every guy I meet
And we never even went on a date

It's hard to start over
When we were so close to the finish line
I hate how our temporary forever
Now only amounts to wasted time

It's hard to start over
When I write every poem about you
You've probably long forgotten about me

But you'll always be my muse

It's hard to start over for me
And I wonder if it's hard for you too

K.G.H.

Nineteen

It's an odd place to be
The age of nineteen
Where I am on the verge of everything
And yet I have nothing

What do I do?
Where do I go?
I'm just a kid
How do they expect me to know?

I spent my whole life wanting to grow up
But now I don't want to let go

K.G.H.

Thanksgiving Dinner

I feel like an adult in a world of children
I feel like a child in a world of adults
I'm out of place, yet in every place
All of my cousins are younger than I
So I can only be seen as a babysitter
Or one of the adults
But to the adults I'm a child too
Yet not a cute child who is praised for every miniscule
thing that they do
Rather the one who has outgrown such adornment
And is asked to fulfill every task
So they can focus on the younger ones

I don't enjoy the games like they do
Like I used to
But I can't relate to the conversations
About corporate bosses and taxes
I knew this time would come
A time where I would have nowhere to sit
No place to fit into
Without sticking out like a sore thumb
I am too big to sit at the children's table
The chairs are too small and my knees stick out

And yet I do not fit in with the grown-ups either
They pour their wine and pat my head

Shall I stand and eat between the two tables?
I can observe both from such a place
I can hear the children laughing and talk about
What they want Santa Claus to bring them
For Christmas this year
Then I can turn my ear to the other side of the room
And I'll hear the adults speak of day-to-day life and
politics

I might as well take notes, after all
If it's who I am to become
I feel pulled in both directions
And yet I feel as if both are repelling against me
Until I am suffocated by the reality that I cannot
control
I thought it was hard to be young
And I know it's hard to grow old
But I think the worst part
Is having no seat to call your own

K.G.H.

Everything that Never Happened

We never went on a date
Although you had planned on it
You asked me a few times but
I didn't know I liked you yet

We never kissed
Although you wanted to
You told me after that car ride
It was all you wanted to do

We never said we loved each other
We never got the chance
We didn't make it far enough
To indulge in our forbidden romance

We never held each other
Just another thing that I hate
You liked me since the day I met you
And I liked you when it was too late

I don't know what I'm supposed to do
Caught in the middle of something new
I never liked a boy until I met you

Never felt a connection so real and true

And I'm the one who broke it off
After you broke me, I couldn't stomach the loss
You wanted to leave the door open
But I'm scared that's just another promise waiting to
be broken

I think of you most every day
Your jokes, your kindness, the way you loved my name
In those long, lonely days I wish you would've called
I wish you would've done something valiant
Or anything at all

Do you stay up at night wondering where it all went
wrong?
Constantly debating if we made a mistake, if this
torment should be prolonged?
I didn't know I gave you permission to make me bleed
I hate how now you're just a bitter memory

I wish you had been true to your word
I wish you had treated me the way I deserved
I hate how I remember more than I imagined

Now you're just everything that never happened

K.G.H.

No Queen Bows Twice

You never loved me
You loved my availability
Eight to ten, you'd book your session
Would my naive heart ever learn its lesson?

A battle brews in my heart
As the troops prepare to mobilize
A war between what I want to believe
And the truth that would be my demise

What a liberator you would've been
Had you cut me loose
I was wrapped around your finger
And it tightened like a noose

To play me like you did
Must've taken up all your time
And here I was jealous
Of the girl I thought you idolized

You call me to the podium
Second place, I take the prize
How did I not know?

You always said that silver matched my eyes

Perhaps your lack of respect
Made me claim my own
It exposed you as the coward
And crowned me to the throne

Now I am free from you
A wounded soldier leaving the fight
You ask me to come back
But my guns are empty tonight

One day someone will love me
The way that I loved you
Willing to jump in the fire
And apologize for getting bruised

One day you will know
Just how it feels
To receive someone's love
And learn it was never real

To feel the emptiness
Of not being wanted

To crave their sickening touch
Even if it's haunted

I wish you had never wasted my time
So I could've stayed the girl
That was unaware
Of such a heart-wrenching crime

Give me back my innocence that you took away
I was once a girl with a childlike heart
But now I am a soldier who struggles
To keep her attackers at bay

The freedom I had
To love and be loved
Lies lifeless on the floor
And there is so much blood

Am I a toy to you?
Was my love for you a game?
I am no longer willing to bend
For a boy who won't change

You broke me and used me

Just for your crooked pleasure
But what a beautiful thing it is
That diamonds form under pressure

Here I am glowing
The finest of jewels
Dissected by your pickaxe
Callous and cruel

I was never yours to shatter
Though you struck like I was stone
I bent until I nearly broke
Just to feel like I was known

Now that you've shown your true colors
I can finally be free
Of a hollow jester
Who doesn't come close to deserving me

Goodbye forever!
I'm happy to say I won't miss you
You say that I'll regret this
But I think we both know that isn't true

I am very thankful for this lesson
To never settle for a temporal, deceitful affair
Now tell me,
Is that a transgression?

Maybe this catastrophe wasn't in vain
And none of this could have been done without you
The woman I became

A woman who knows
How lucky she is
To be free from a man
Who didn't know what he had
When he had it

Stronger now
I will move on
And focus on loving myself
Now that you're gone

I am excited to see
What the future brings
A queen right now
Who will one day meet a king

Who will love me more
Than you ever could
And treat me in the way
That a king should

And if you ever crawl back–
By Her Majesty's royal decree:
You'll draw your last breath
Beneath my guillotine

K.G.H.

The Clearing

∿

She wasn't healed
but she could breathe
and that was something

Breathe

I am a human being
My imperfections are proof of it
I am alive
My mistakes dismantle the alternative
Of what is imaginary
And seemingly perfect
Its darling flaw
Is its lack of existence
What is dead
Does not have the opportunity for failure
Nor the ceiling

Of laughter that aches the stomach
Or tears derived from joy that cannot be satisfied by
words alone
Nor the simplest inhale and exhale

My soul beats blood in my chest
And my spirit sends signals throughout my skeleton

Yet there are those who ponder
The existence of a creator
Who created humans in His image

With the palette to create
In a severed mirror of our sculptor
Offers flexibility for devastation
And the very sense of what it means to truly live

To breathe is to fall
To breathe is to try
To breathe is to grasp
To breathe is to be alive

So just breathe

K.G.H.

Everything All at Once

It's okay to be everything all at once

Or a little bit of this here

And a little bit of that there

Because the truth is

We don't have enough time

To be everything we want to be

In this life

K.G.H.

Just Say Something

Say something stupid

Say something risky

Say something shockingly true

Just say something

And say it now

Before I crawl back into my cocoon of indifference

And cut off my wings of courage

K.G.H.

Live Like You're Dying

Would you live in a different way
If you were told you would die today
The truth is we all die someday
We get closer as we age
We aren't promised another time
Another chance, another sunrise
Let's not wait until it's too late
And everyone cries
To do the things we love most
And make us feel alive

Would you tell your family you loved them
And do everything you could
To right all the wrongs in your life
That you always knew you should

Live like you're dying
Because you are

K.G.H.

Colorblind

Maybe I didn't show you my true colors
Because you cannot see rainbows
You are colorblind to anything good and true
You have fallen victim to the numbness
And blindness of the world
So you do not hear the music I dance to
Nor see the stars in my sky
You can't feel the breeze I sway in
Or smell the freshness of nature
That astounds me
So why would I bother
Inviting you into a world
That you cannot enter?
To you, everything is black and white
So that is all you see
I only see bright palettes
And I let them consume me
Because you do not understand my world
You make fun of me
But it is you
Whose senses fail
And deprive you of the very things
That mean anything in this life

I may look like a fool
But at least I do not think like one
I'd rather dance like an idiot
Than restrict myself from life's fun

K.G.H.

Facing the Wave

My legs grow tired
My fears are a tsunami raging after me

It isn't until I stop
And turn around
That I see what I've been running from
What I let it grow into

I cannot keep running
So I face it
And let it wash over me

It is only when I am brave enough
To face my fears
That I become strong enough
To be enough

When all that remains
Is what hadn't washed away–
The trembling creature rises
And finally gets the chance
To start fresh
To create a new destiny

From here
It is only up
And she won't take
A single moment for granted

Thank you, tsunami
You didn't ruin me
You refined me
By showing me
That if my greatest fears cannot destroy me
Then surely nothing can

K.G.H.

Awake and Overdue

Oh, how badly I want to feel
I want to experience all of it
Every human emotion
Every piece of evidence that I am alive
That my soul exists and has free will
I yearn and I ache
For an overwhelming climax of feelings
That the world has taught me to oppress
And shove back where it came from
Like a jack-in-the-box
I feel so deeply when I remember to
We are numbed to death
By devices with bright screens
Connected to our hands by
A magnetic force
And the perception of ourselves that
We were told to idolize above authenticity
Why must we continue to follow a rubric made
By nothing divine
And nothing more
Than mere human beings
Who wept and fell and looked to the sky
And questioned their very breath?

Why must we suppress our passions to be exalted and desired?
It's killing me from the inside out
I can no longer live a life of indifference
I am a volcano thousands of years overdue
And it is time to erupt

K.G.H.

Neither Here Nor There

You'll get there

But right now you're here

And if you keep taking life as it comes

One moment at a time

Then one day

The "there" that you were so obsessed with

That felt out of reach and a million miles away

Will be "here"

It will be now and you will want to get somewhere else

A new "here"

A new dream

And that's okay

Perfectly normal

But don't you forget

That you made it there

K.G.H.

The Gift of Thorns

A thorn in my side
I pleaded three times
To remove my burden
And bring glory to His name

But instead of sparing my pain
He parted the sea and made a way
For within my weakness I rely on Him
A Father who loves His daughter and hates her sin

I envy myself once as a child
Beautiful, brave, bold, and wild
Yet now I'm a feeble and breakable woman
Aren't we supposed to progress with age?

But now I see my thorn as a gift
Because without it
I would not feel the urgency of running to Him
And surrendering all for His glory

I shall seek His face more than His hand
Take my treasures and leave my depravity of man
If my reliance on You depends on my weakness

I will count it all joy
As it leads me to Jesus

K.G.H.

Just Like That

I tell myself I don't like you

But I keep waiting for you to text me back

It's funny how nothing can turn into something

Just like that

K.G.H.

My Reality

What is reality?

How I view life is merely my perception of it

A cognitive bias

A customized lens, one of its kind

Made only to fit my eyes, my mind, my soul

Things make sense to me in a way they don't for most

A puzzle cut into different pieces for each individual player

My brain subconsciously takes notes

How will I view this life?

My precepts are up for the taking

Forged every day under trial and by fire

Deciding who I will be

And how I perceive this world, this life

My reality is different from everyone else's

Even those whom I share close quarters

Or am alike by nature

I could have the same life as someone

Mirror their movements

And match their steps but

It's all about perception

And what you believe

How you see things and view things
And choose to accept or alter things

This person in an alternate reality
Could love their every breath
And smile at every failure
Viewing it as proof of their rare ability to be human
While the pessimistic side of myself
Views safety as terror
And mistakes toothy smiles for fangs

It's not even about what's real anymore
It's how we choose to see it
And what we believe about it
Through my eyes
What I let into my heart and mind
That fluctuates in my soul
How will I view this life!?

If I want to see magic everywhere then I will
And if I want to see failure, fear, and embarrassment
everywhere then I will
Lost potential will not be discarded on my account
No, I see it clearly now

There are no missed expectations
But instead beautiful, yet fleeing opportunities
Every single day
To be who I want to be
In a world however I choose to see it

Is the rain an inconvenience or is it sent to help me
grow?
A free shower from the sky
To wash off all my false, dirty perceptions of this life
A loss only creates space for more beauty, does it not?
I want to see sparkles and sunshines and giggles and joy

So I think I will
That can be my reality

K.G.H.

Silently Yours

I see you all the way across the room
While my eyes secretly wander, I notice yours never do
You would think that my stares make an obvious clue
Have you not seen the way I look at you?

Can you see into my fervid eyes?
Are they transparent or do you only see baby blue
skies?

And if you ever were to pick my brain
And feel my blood flow within my veins
And hear the beating of my heart
You would know that I've always loved you, right from
the very start

K.G.H.

I Am in My Freaking Twenties

I seem to have forgot

And I don't know why

But now I've remembered

I am in my twenties

I'm not two months in but

I am in my twenties

The time of my life

That used to be so far away

The time of my life

That I should be having the time of my life

I am in my twenties

I am in my freaking twenties

K.G.H.

The Unknown

I always thought the unknown was scary
Because of its wide range of outcomes
But that is also what makes it so thrilling
We don't fear success, love, and happiness
But on the latter–rejection, pain, loss, and regret
However, I wouldn't want it any other way
How boring it would be
And how rattling
I would already know my triumphs with no heroic
unveil
And I would dread my inevitable defeat
Until my life drifted into the wind
Forgotten such as the common weed
I am thankful to not know what my future holds
What a blessing it is
The unknown

K.G.H.

The Ache of Arrival

I have found a gut-wrenching truth

Sitting in the dream I once strived and scrapped for

I ache for who I once was

The daily mundane

The familiar ebb and flow of the climb

And now that I am here

And the adventure is over

The journey is complete

The

     journey

         is

          complete.

                K.G.H.

Before the Music Ends

Wear your favorite perfume
And your fancy jewelry
And dance the way you like to
You woke up today
And tomorrow you might not
Life is a special occasion
The present is exactly what it claims to be
Do it now and enjoy it properly and fully
Instead of waiting for the moon to align with the sun
Smile and sing and laugh before it's too late
And time takes away all that we've become

K.G.H.

A Cinematic Moment

Watching the rain
Might be my favorite thing to do
Sitting in the presence
Of God's creation mightily at work
Is a holy thing indeed

The scene is an August afternoon–
Cloudy and warm
But with a breeze that makes me grab a blanket
The rain is trickling ever so lightly
I hear it at a constant on the tin roof
Every contender of this masterpiece is meant to be here
Nothing is out of place
Nothing is missing
Everything is present
The sounds
The scenery
The feeling of contentment, nostalgia, and hope for
what is to come
All at the same time

The sun is not out
But it is bright enough to know it isn't far

There is green everywhere
The grass
The trees
The plants
The weeds
The color green in nature means life
And here it is so lively
The rain is nurturing the ground
As the blue helps the other colors
The other life
I hear birds chirping
And singing songs to one another
Such a beautiful sound

A nostalgic sense of childhood and simplicity
Has entered the scene
This moment is bittersweet
A cinematic moment if you will
A moment that you are lucky to experience
Just once in your life
A moment you love so much
That it hurts
Because you know it will come to an end
And only be a memory

A moment of the past
And gone forever
Only to be lost between the pages of history books
And hang on the tips of dead men's lips

But until then
I sit in awe and full of bliss
A delight only obtained
Through the simplest moments of life
Moments that cannot be
Rushed
Created
Or even planned
But one where all you can do is fall into
And hope to soak it all up before it vanishes

They aren't big enough to talk about
And pictures will never do them justice
But to know a moment is yours
And only yours
For however brief it may be
Makes it incredibly sacred
It can only be captured with your senses
And stored in your memories

In a world of runners
I choose to sit
And appreciate the beauty of this moment

A moment where the birds sing
And the bugs hum
Where the rain has stopped
But the dew remains as proof of what was
Where my dad drives his green truck
To the barn and checks on the cows
Where I put my headphones on
And listen to classical piano
That I hope to play one day
I tune out everything else
Because this is my moment
A moment where the wind chimes play
And remind me of my grandmother
When we would sit on her front porch swing
And talk endlessly
Where we would listen to storms
And watch the rain
Much like I have today

Listening to beautiful keys

With no expectations
Once long ago
And now as me
Between a woman and a child
This scene could be considered picturesque
To a hopeless romantic
Like myself
Where I read about a world
That does not exist
And form connections with characters
I will never meet
And disappear into their world temporarily
An alluring balance of actuality

The bugs are louder now
And the breeze has died down
Just because this moment has changed
Does not make it any less whole
It evolves
And continues on
As do I

Nostalgia
Contentment

And hope

A happy childhood memory

A peace of mind

And an excitement of the unknown

Combined

Into

A cinematic moment

K.G.H.

The Unfurling

To shed old skins
is to plant new seeds

Gentle Persistence

Impatience is greedy

She says to hurry up

Because where you are

And what you have

Isn't enough

But patience is content

Though she still has dreams

And yearns to be someone else

Some place else

She does so with ease

She does so with a smile

A calm mind

And a joyful spirit

Because what she has is more than enough

The unknown is just a mystery

She will not fear it

She's reminded of where she used to be

And with fortitude she made it here

So she knows

That one day

Oh, one day

She will make it

It may take days

But she's willing to wait years

She knows the waiting is worth it

It is because it has to be

Nothing worth having ever comes easy

And is as rare as a fish in a tree

On the hard days

When impatience crumbles

Patience is tough

She doesn't have all the answers

But for now

Today is enough

K.G.H.

Same Things

I've come to find

That often times

Our biggest fears

And greatest dreams

Happen to be

The same things

K.G.H.

Outgrown

My room is outdated

My clothes are too small

I've abandoned ideals I once conspired

My childhood drawings tattoo the wall

But the artist in me has new dreams now

It is time to break through the safety of my cocoon

And dare to fly

I yearn for new places

And new faces

These don't fit me anymore

This land ties me to expectations of who I once was

But I'm no longer that girl

So I wear her clothes

And live in her room

And since we have the same face

It's easy to pretend

But they don't see the groaning

And the agony

Of living a life

That I've outgrown

It's time to pack my bags and move on

It's time to let go

K.G.H.

Like a Wizard

I like how I laugh when I'm with you

It's not forced or fake or muffled

It's real and giggly and pretty even

It reminds me of being a child with stars in my eyes

When I couldn't help but laugh

Because everything was so magical

And that's what you are to me

Full of magic

Like a wise wizard with a big, pointy hat

Now tell me, how could I not laugh at something like that?

K.G.H.

When the Leaves Fall

I hope when I fall

It is as bittersweet and as graceful

As the leaves that turn on the tree

Which remind me

That endings can be beautiful too

K.G.H.

Jonah

When I run away from You, Lord
Out of pure disobedience
To satisfy my mortal flesh
I do not even consider
The intricacy of Your plan
Only my mere happiness
If I must sacrifice my pride
To adhere to Your will
I must be refined to the image of Your Son
To have a faith of steel
Because what You ask of me
My flesh yearns to say no
But Lord, wherever You call me
I will go

K.G.H.

When You Stop Fighting

I found an abundance of eudaimonia–
A plethora of purpose
When I stopped trying to be who I once was
And finally embraced the girl that I've become
She's pretty great
If I would let her be
And stop comparing her
To a girl that I fought so hard
To unbecome

When you change
Don't be surprised when you change
Don't freak out about it either
I think you'll find a lot more peace
And a lot more joy
And do a lot more living
When you put away your boxing gloves
And get to know the girl in the mirror

You fought so hard to be her
Now it's time to stop fighting her

K.G.H.

The Gardener of My Heart

My sin is a great, thick weed
Even without the right living conditions
It refuses to die

But still–
He holds the clouds
He is patient
He waits

And after what seems like a lifetime
The weed begins to wither and wilt

I look up at the sky in anger
Why, God, why?
Why would You allow my fruits to die?

But they were never fruits
Only the overgrowth of a heart
Too intertwined in sin to see clearly

I mistook it for myself
But it is the part of me
That needs to die

How loving
How gracious
How merciful
How good is my God

That in my sin
He loves me
He pursues me
He has a plan for me

Only a good father
Takes away what harms His child
Even when she can't see it
Even when she doesn't believe or understand
Even when it breaks her

God is refining me
Pruning me
Purifying me
Into the image of Jesus

Thank you, God
For being the gardener of my heart
For killing what would have destroyed me

And giving me a fresh start

K.G.H.

Defying the Queen

Freedom finally came
When I defied the tyrant in my head

The moment the world didn't end
Her threats lost their power
And I gained mine

K.G.H.

Conformity's Canvas

How sadistic it is

That a piece of art

Is its own greatest adversary

Its most adorned critic

For not being another composition

Watercolor wishes it were stencil

And charcoal envies acrylic paint

Not one seldom complains about its medium

And they all long to be admired

But how can one commend a work of art that does not embrace its unique qualities?

The internal struggle is seen in the brushstrokes

Crafted to admonish the notion that beauty lies in conformity

And instead, intrinsic value is not based upon its allegiance to uniform

But the artist didn't long for normalcy in His work

He envisioned world-altering, awe-inspiring, heart-clenching beauty

The creation, by its own hand, sabotaged the destiny that once awaited it

Because it was obsessed with being what it was not

Something that it could never be

Instead of focusing on

What it was

And what it was created to be

Yes, some may gawk at its existence

For they will not understand its design

But it was not created for everyone

Its purpose was something divine

K.G.H.

Would You Live For Me?

Dying is easy
Living is hard
Ending myself as a loving martyr
Would be an escape from the pain
But to live for someone is a slow death
Only unconditional love remains

Dying is dramatic
But it's done in an instant
It doesn't test your patience
Or stretch your limits
It doesn't require strenuous dedication
While it is a sacrifice
Living is choosing to show up for someone
Every day of your life

Staying–
That's the harder thing
It's listening when I'm exhausted
Apologizing when I'm hurt
Being kind when I feel anything but
Offering grace you didn't earn
It's carrying your weight

When I can barely lift my own
Remembering the little things
To make you feel known
Waking up every morning
To thank the Lord and pray
Then do it all again
Without being asked
And choosing to love you anyway

To live for someone
Means to stay
When it would be easier to go
To not just fall in love
But to nurture it and watch it grow

You say that you would die for me
And you would gladly bleed
But would you hold the weight of my world
And still decide to breathe?

K.G.H.

I Don't Care

Am I cringy?
That's okay
I wasn't trying to fit into your
Fleeting, unreachable box of perfection anyway

I don't care in a freeing way
Not a numbing one
Aren't we all doing our best
Under the same sun?

K.G.H.

No More Masks

I wake up and prepare to start my day
I cannot forget my mask as I walk out the door
My uniform, my demeanor, my disguise

I wonder if someone would truly look into my eyes
If they would see who is inside the body
That walks around daily and does as it's told
The soul of a girl longing for more
And to be free of societal norms

Why is it profound
To hide our feelings?
Why must we wear a mask
With a fake face
Gleaming with counterfeit pride
Maybe if we did what we loved
We would not have to hide

And isn't it silly
That we worry so much
About the opinions of people
Who don't even care about us?

What a regret I will have
At the end of my life
If I continue down this path
Of unconscious people-pleasing
To the point of such sacrifice
That I lose myself in the process

I am tired of this constant state of anxiety
That clouds on top of me
I would rather be considered absurd to others
Than a coward to myself

I want to run to the top of a hill and scream
And not wonder what the people below think of me
I want to do what I want to do
I am sick at the thought of being controlled
By the opinions of people
Who do not have opinions of value to me

I want to grow a garden
And raise chickens
And make homemade pasta
And play the piano
And write poetry

And novels
And dance and sing and smile and laugh
And hug and love and live life
With the utmost sincerity and joy

I want to be who I was created to be
The woman that I was saved to be
And not be chained to the unattainable and fleeing
expectations
Of a fallen world that I don't belong to anyway

What a tragedy it would be
To live my life
And yet never be me

                                        K.G.H.

I Can Smile

The more I grow up
The more I realize
That I just want to be me
Sometimes I want to hide and no one know me
Sometimes I just want the person in front of me to
know me
And sometimes I want the whole world to know me
I think it's more freeing that way
You either love me or you don't
But I don't have to wonder
I can smile
And you can frown
But I can smile
I can finally smile

K.G.H.

Like a Child

The wind chimes on your grandmother's porch
The backyard swing
The dog that got ran over
The doll that sings

Nights at the fair
Backseat rides
Trips to the beach
Big, sappy smiles

The lunch table laughs
With your middle school friends
Little did you know
You'd never see them again

The days of dress-up
And swimming in the pool
Walking past your crush
And trying to be cool

Sleepover giggles
And playing outside
Barefoot in the dark

Chasing fireflies

Snow day highs
Nighttime lullabies
Popsicles when it's hot
Hot chocolate when it's not

Bike rides
Pinky promises
Secret handshakes
Innocent accomplices

Staying up late
Thinking you're so sneaky
The next morning you realize your parents were right
And you're oh so sleepy

The innocence of childhood
The negligence of responsibility
I wish I could go back in time
To a life of such simplicity

To giggle at mundane things
And not seek constant praise

When did I lose the color
That once lit up my days?

It's ironic how badly
I wanted to grow
Not knowing what I'd have to give up
Later down the road

But here I am
Beaten down with so much stress
Checking every box
Except the one marked "happiness"

I'm tired of letting my life pass me by
What would my younger self say?
Could she look me in the eye?

She dreamed luminous dreams
And believed in me
I seem to have lost her
Or misplaced the key

I hate how I shrink for others
How validation drives me

It's my life to live
Not for strangers to foresee

Maybe I don't have
To be a kid again
To live authentically
I don't have to play pretend

A wake-up call
I will not dismiss
I don't want to forget these days
As they will be the ones I'll miss

Just like now, looking back
I will see there is nothing I lack
Material things will never satisfy
Rather the love of others and the words we live by

I think it's funny how
I never thought I was pretty
But looking upon pictures
I realize I was my own worst enemy

I envy who I once was

But doesn't that show
How even after all these years
I won't allow myself to grow?

I want to be present
Like a flower in bloom
Not wasting away
In a self-made tomb

Life is only as bright
As the lens you choose
You can live in the shadows
Or embrace the vibrant hues

God has blessed me with so much
My life is a gift
Is there a better way to honor the Lord
Than to truly live it?

Who says growing up
Means dampening your spark?
Why can't we be wise
And still dance in the dark?

I think the world
Would be a much better place
If we didn't grow up in our hearts
I think there would be a lot more grace

The kindness of a child
Still lives in me
Despite the world's weight
That's who I choose to be

Today I decide to reminisce
On my past with a smile
But just because I am a grown-up
Does not mean that I cannot live like a child

K.G.H.

The Garden

Let her grow unrestrained
like a beautiful flower
wild and untamed

I Am Meant For More

I can no longer pretend
That I am a caterpillar
When I am truly
An unruly butterfly

I cannot keep cutting
Off my wings
To blend into
A society of dirt and branches
And grubs that crawl and moan

It hurts to kill
The parts of myself
That tempt me to dare
And lead me into a destiny
Beyond my limited horizon

I must let my wings flourish
Along with the bold characteristics
Of the woman that I sincerely am
Even if it means
Disrupting those who cannot fly

I cannot shrink
Into the position and the space
That the world prepared for me long ago
When I was a child and they placed
A fixed map in my hands
And a predetermined fate in my heart

I will not cripple my potential in fear of offending
I must live veraciously and stop pretending
That I am less than I am
In fear of rejection
I cannot conceal my true form
For compliant, conformist connection

Do I dare flee from purpose, from destiny, now that I
have awoken?
Do I yearn for a life unfulfilled, discontent, and
broken?
No, it is time for I
To spread my wings
Unapologetically
And make a life in the sky

The shrieks cannot force me into cowardice

The scoffs cannot lead me down the wide road
Of misery and societal enormities
For a weakling's sake, doing as one's told

I have to soar
I long to fly
I must embrace my disposition
Or I will surely die

I will heed the call towards the Heavens
Even if I meet Icarus's fate
At least I have the courage to chase meaning and
freedom
Before the hourglass runs out of sand to shake

I refuse to falter
My calling is much too high
I was not meant to dwell in the soil
I was made for the sky

Let the Earth weep for what it could not keep
You may shout my name in threats so deep
But your curses are as good as mute
As I cannot hear them from above

Purpose does not need permission
To live the life that one loves

K.G.H.

The Permission Was Always Mine

I waited years

For permission to be happy

In my body

And my skin

And my mind

And my choices

And my purpose

And my flaws

And my life

I just didn't know that I was the only one

Who could bestow it

To grant myself such freedom

And pardon me from a life

Of misery and shame

And let me just say

It feels so good

Like an elephant taking its foot off my chest

To finally take a deep breath

To smile in the face of fear

And dance down the streets of indifference

The only approval you need is your own

K.G.H.

The Rarest Thing Is Right now

Oh, just look around!

These are the very moments that you will remember
one day

And how they were filled with magic

And oozing with laughter and love

You woke up today!

Create new memories

Forge destiny with your very fingers

Draw a grin on your face

And dance like you've always wanted to

These are the days!

These are the days that people dream about

These are the days that you will one day dream about

Even after you get your dream

Life isn't about what happens once you get the dream

And fulfill the prophecy

Life is about who you become

And the memories you make on the way there

The fire in your eyes

The strength in your soul

The joy in your step
And the love in your heart
For the people and the place that surrounds you

It will all be over entirely too soon
Please soak it all up
And don't leave a drop of life unlived
Fully, truly, completely, purposefully, passionately
What is life, if not lived in this way?
You are a gift to the world
And the world has given you a gift in exchange

Oh, would you just look around
And inside of you too?
There is magic everywhere
And in everything you do
Look at how lucky we are
And just think of how rare any of this is
The ability to love and create and try again
The ability to breathe and live

Oh, just look around
And maybe you would see
How your worldly problems disappear

When you realize what a miracle it is
Just to be

K.G.H.

The Jump

I saw the crazed expression on your face

When I told you I was going to jump

I guess it never occurred to you

That I was going to fly

K.G.H.

Springtime

I love springtime
Even if it doesn't always love me back
And if it weren't for how I can never tell
If I'm falling apart or just allergic to the air
It would be my favorite season
But summer asks fewer questions

So anyway–springtime

I love seeing the sun hang around a little longer each
day
I love seeing vibrant green slowly overtake nature again
I love hearing the insects sing in unison when the
moon comes out
I love how it's warm enough for shorts in the afternoon
And chilly in the morning still

But most of all
I love how spring reminds me that life constantly
changes
And even after a dark winter
Things will become lovely again

K.G.H.

Chess Pie

I want my life to be rich

Not like fancy cars and vacation houses

But rich like chess pie

It's easy to make

And plain as can be

Whoever is lucky enough to get a taste

Always leaves with a full belly

It's so full of sweetness that you can't eat it all at once

It seems that it could last forever

And one bite is more than enough

K.G.H.

The Burden of Being Perfect

My whole life I've been a perfectionist
Where success is expected, not an earned victory
Entirely stubborn and habitually hardheaded
My father in feminine form

And yet I have found another trait of mine
That forces a standstill inside me
I must be perfect
And I must be in control

But how can I be faultless, as a mortal?
A human being's design is flawed and fatal

And so the battle rages–
Will she even begin if she cannot craft
Her desired outcome with flawless precision?

Another vial is emptied into the cauldron
A hypersensitive girl who demands perfection of
herself
Would be quite bored without a hobby

She must obsess over the opinions of others

And crave their validation and acceptance
Like a vampire to fresh blood

Filling herself with worldly schemes
And temporal distractions
Does not mix with divine purpose

Fleshful desires
Do not accumulate
With a heavenly will

Redundant and baleful
A waste of time
Spent revolving in circles
That were never meant to be entertained

Giving God space to be Himself
Is the only way to have peace
In this breakneck society

Surrender means
Changing our heart's posture
Changing our goal from
A desired outcome

To genuine obedience

Without trial
There are no lessons to be learned
No opportunity to trust
To overcome
To prevail

Without facing an immovable mountain
And being humbled within my human limitation
How would I see the true glory of God?
How else would I feel Him carry my lifeless body
Through valleys and over mountains?

My thorns force me into an inevitable predicament
My unyielding spirit tires as all my attempts fail
To hold the world in my hands
Is to be crushed by its weight

I bear Atlas's punishment as self-imposed duty
God puts the globe in my hands as I ask unrelenting
Against my better judgement, my corpse is obliterated
Leaving only a desperate soul pierced with shame

Surrender is the art of le t t i n g g o
Of what is not mine to manage
True surrender is letting life simply happen
And trust that nothing surprises the Lord–
Which it doesn't

It is trusting that He has a plan
Exceedingly greater and higher
Than the most agrestal dreams I possess

Only then can I be okay with
Whatever outcome is bestowed
Because even wooly paths can lead to a fruitful oasis
A dirt trail may diverge from the crowd
But has untouched beauty
Only witnessed by the sets of eyes
That are open to appreciate it

It is a beautiful thing
To trust in the Lord
Fully, completely, blindly

And how are we blind to His goodness
When Love was nailed to a cross in our stead?

He has the resume and all authority to work through
us
If we only let Him
And who am I to deny the Lord entry in His own
temple?

I will lay at His feet
And empty my perfume there
I will empty my heart also
Of my burdens, my pride, my will

Control is not mine to keep
The price too high
The climb too steep

The lies of Satan have clawed at my neck
For far too long
How liberating a fleeing
To prove he is wrong

I will not attempt to control every aspect
Of everyone and everything around me
Does a captain try to control his vessel
Or does he try to control the sea?

To be a child
Is to be taken care of
And there is no greater Father
Than mine

The burden of being perfect
Is one I will no longer hold
It is time to trust in the One
Who is perfectly in control

K.G.H.

I'm Not One to Long for Pain

I'm not one to long for pain
But when you leave and I am left alone
I don't mind the emptiness that the room indulges in
It is proof you were once here

I'm not one to long for pain
But your jokes are just too funny
My stomach has no choice but to betray my senses and
twist into knots
A sweet agony that I cannot escape

I'm not one to long for pain
But I'd rather fight with you than win the prize of
loneliness
I would choose to argue with you than be agreeable
with anyone else
I don't care what we do, as long as it's together

I'm not one to long for pain
But for you
That is a burden I would gladly take

K.G.H.

With You

My life has two phases:
Before you
And with you

And everything is so much brighter
With you in it

K.G.H.

My Comeback

I like to imagine my comeback
As the slightest bit of light
Shining over the horizon
After the coldest, darkest, scariest night

The temperature was well below freezing
And I was ill-prepared for such weather
It was so dark that not even the moon
Dared to show its face

I couldn't see a step in front of me
I could only hear the sounds
The rustling in the woods
The howling in the distance
The crackling of the branches

I was so paralyzed with fear
And not only so
But I thought that my body would give out
If not slaughtered

I saw no way forward
And no way out

But then–
Oh, then–
I could make out
The outline of my shoes

I thought I was hallucinating
That the frostbite had gotten to my brain
That it was time
For nature to take its course

But it was true–
There was light

And as time went on
It only got brighter
And the sun brought warmth
That healed my body
As it stopped shivering

I could finally see all the beauty
That was hidden in the night

And the howling stopped
As the dogs went to rest

And I was no longer bothered by the rustling
Or terrified of what I could not see

To come out on the other side
Is a liberating thing

—

I see my comeback
As a dry and barren land

It had not been fruitful in so long
That all the farmers had given up on it
Even the stubborn ones

They saw it as worthless
They thought it would never be plentiful
Like it once used to
It was left to decay

And yet
In spite of it all
There was a blossom
A sprout

A small plant

It could easily be plucked out
Or eaten by a hungry animal
And nothing more would come of it
Except that it did

With each passing day
The sun shone graciously upon it
And in return
The soil relentlessly fought
As the clouds watered it
And the dust disappeared

The grass became a vibrant green
And it grew thick and taller by the day
And beautiful flowers bloomed

Which everyone thought was odd because
No one had ever planted flowers there before
Flowers of unspeakable and marvelous color
Consumed the field

They blew effortlessly in the wind

Yet did not break
And every time someone passed by
They couldn't help but be inspired
And smile
And wonder

Where such beauty had come from
And how it bloomed
In the most desolate of circumstances

Magical things can grow
When life is kind enough
To offer second chances

K.G.H.

Dirty Dishes

There are dishes on the counter
And the house is a mess
But one day it will be clean
And I will be a guest

So I don't mind the clutter
I appreciate it really
It shows the familiarity and comfort we share
You don't have to clean up to impress me

I dread the day when you will say
"We need to clean the house, Gracie is on her way"
Like it wasn't my home not too long ago
I dread the day that won't be so

Not because of the beautiful wooden beams
Or the breathtaking view out the window
But because I won't be with you every day
You will no longer be just down the hallway

So please don't worry
When the house is dirty
Because if it isn't homey

It is often very lonely

And if I had to choose
Between one or the other
I would choose the messiest of houses
With my loving mother

K.G.H.

Is This What Healing Feels Like?

How is it possible

To feel peace within my pain?

Is this–

Is this what healing feels like?

K.G.H.

I Hope You Follow Your Dreams

I hope that one day you're on a plane

Sitting in the window seat

I hope you get to see the city lights from thousands of feet up

And realize how small the world really is

I hope that wherever you're going

It's far away from here

I hope you have the courage to do that

To leave it all behind

In the pursuit of becoming who you are

I hope you don't cry

I hope you smile

I hope you're not afraid

And if you are, I hope you do it anyway

I hope you're brave enough to fight for the life you want

Instead of hiding from its consequences

I hope you travel the world

And see new sights

And cities

And cultures

And people

And places

And I hope it brings you the joy you always thought it
would
I hope it gives you freedom and purpose and pleasure
And memories that carry you forever
I hope you become better because of it
And I hope you allow yourself to be happy
To have fun
To be wild
And do what you want to do for once
Without a second thought for other people
And their opinions
I hope you get to live your dream
And not just dream about it
And once you do
I hope you have the courage
To chase after something new

K.G.H.

She Would Finally Fly

From the moment she was born
She was different from everyone around her
She didn't laugh to fill the silence
Or clap when she wasn't entertained
She always lived deliberately and authentically
And since she did so
She always thought that everyone else did too

Life wears on a woman over time
She was no different–
For once
As she got older
She fell into the routine
Of being a mechanical machine
She smiled on command
And fit in with her peers
She had a life of success
As the others said
Laid out and hers for the taking

Would anyone else consider
Hitting rock bottom a blessing
Other than she?

New to the world as a woman
She found herself lost
And more hopeless than ever
Who had she become?
It wasn't until she was emptied
Of the trash the world had fed her
That she could come back home to herself
She began to see colors
And dancing and laughter all around
She was free, at last

She found it odd
That the people who claimed to love her
Were the same ones who tried to chain her
Why were they so bothered
By her being herself?
Why couldn't they let her be happy?

Everything changed when she realized
She didn't need their permission to be happy
Only her own
At least she had the courage to fly
They could laugh
But she would fly

She would finally fly

K.G.H.

To Live Untamed is to Die Free

I find solace in the dirt
Sitting above it and not buried under it
Running atop with feet light as a feather
Standing tall with a heart as heavy as stone
What a reckless conundrum, such an interesting
juxtaposition
An attempt to live life at present with the knowledge of
growing old
I am acutely aware of where I will go
I must keep my blood hot before my heart grows cold
Before it all goes dark and my beloved surround me
with woe
Before time takes me, I must try it all
Be it success or slander
At my last breath, at least I'll know

When Death finds me, I pray that he finds me alive
Not sunken, defeated, boring, or just trying to get by
Before my numbered days are through, I hope I muster
the courage it takes to fly
To be a bird in a wingless culture
Above scrutiny, conformity, and false security
To be one with the wind

Finding freedom in an endless sky

I find purpose lying lost in the evergreen
Pondering down the many paths unseen
My mind is one with the inevitable flow of the stream
Here is not to do or die, for here is to dream
Here there are no deadlines, disagreements, or
distractions
There is no tightrope I must straddle to win approval,
awards, and worth
There is no crowd to appease, no pressure to perform
Just a playwright fulfilling her divine destiny
The woodland creatures do not dare tarnish her true,
unscripted form

Sitting in the crook of an old oak, I silently observe fate
as the sun sets
I smell an abundance of pollen, I see the rolling of hills
Time slows as nature begins to rest
It is during the song of the weeds
That I am more consciously alive than I've ever been
My senses heighten, my imagination is untamed
At last, I am a child again

For in this place, my mask has been surrendered to the ground
There is no exhausting façade, only the real and profound
Where there is no need to be a mechanical machine
Flawlessly executing tasks, unfulfilling and mortally deemed

I find peace within the woods
It is here I no longer wonder why
I live deliberately among the trees
Sucking every ounce of marrow out of life

K.G.H.

Acknowledgements

I am thankful to God for giving me the gift and passion to write–for always loving me and never leaving me. El Roi sees me, knows me, and walks beside me. To Him, I owe my life and all glory.

I would also like to thank my little sister, Lily, who was the first person to ever read my poems. Thank you for welcoming my vulnerability and holding it with kindness and excitement.

Without the inspiration of *Dead Poets Society*, my poems of bravery and true freedom would not exist. This film has changed my life, as both a writer and human. It taught me the courage to live deliberately, the urgency of finding my voice, to embrace my passions unapologetically, and to follow my own path–no matter the cost.

I am proud of myself for not giving up and chasing down this mountainous dream. There were countless opportunities to quit and hide in fear, but to survive such a flood and learn how to grow flowers is a strength I'm still amazed to possess.

And lastly, I would like to thank you. Thank you for reading my book, for giving it a chance to change and inspire you. I'm thankful for your support and time. I appreciate it more than you know.

About the author

Kaitlyn Grace Hoagland is a 20-year-old poet from Tennessee. She wrote *Floods and Flowers* between the ages of 18 and 20. This book follows her journey through the pain and beauty of becoming who she's meant to be. This is her debut poetry collection.

Until next time ...